GREAT
GIFT WRAPPING

GREAT GIFT WRAPPING

ELIZABETH LAWRENCE

PRINCE PAPERBACKS
CROWN PUBLISHERS, INC., NEW YORK

A Prince Paperback book. Published by Crown Publishers, Inc., 201 East 50th Street, New York, New York 10022.
Member of the Crown Publishing Group.
Prince Paperbacks and colophon are trademarks of Crown Publishers, Inc.
Manufactured in the United States of America
Book design by Lauren Dong
Illustrations by Jennifer Harper

Library of Congress Cataloging-in-Publication Data
Lawrence, Elizabeth
Great gift wrapping/text and photographs by Elizabeth Lawrence.
1. Gift wrapping. I. Title.
TT870. L33 1991
745.54—dc20   90-27259 CIP

ISBN 0-517-57769-0

10 9 8 7 6 5 4 3 2 1

First Edition

CONTENTS

PART II

GREAT GIFT WRAPPING FOR ALL OCCASIONS

INTRODUCTION

*J*ust as you can't judge a book by its cover, you can't tell a gift from its wrapping. After all, that's the very point of covering it with paper and ribbon.

Although a book requires hours of reading to discover its secrets, a gift must make its most important impression as it is opened. The pleasure of anticipation and the surprise are quickly resolved at the removal of the ribbon and ripping of the paper.

Whether the object inside is an expensive and important gift or only a small token, the skillfully and tastefully wrapped gift can express a great deal. The care and attention you have invested in its wrapping can speak for your affection, appreciation, and friendship. Careful presentation can convey your confidence that the gift is worthy. The thoughtfully wrapped present speaks for your wish to please the recipient.

Wrapping it right can make all the difference. At any stage of life, from childhood through old age, the wrapped package can heighten the excitement of an event. The secret within adds a sense of mystery and wonder: The recipient doesn't know what is inside—it could be almost anything!

The mystery need only be within, however, as there is nothing hard or complicated about perfect presentation when it comes to gift wrapping. Fifty years ago, that wasn't quite so true. Then there was only a limited selection of wrapping goods. For most people, gifts were to be covered with white tissue paper and tied with a bow. Packages were wrapped without the benefit of tape, since it hadn't yet come into general use.

Some of the old ways remain. For example, at Tiffany and Co., the prestigious New York jewelry store, all packages are still wrapped with only ribbon. But the marketplace has changed, as today there is a remarkable array of commercially available papers. There are papers for every imaginable occasion, and of different weights and styles to suit various needs. Some are whimsical, many sentimental and sweet, others sophisticated and sleek.

Ribbons, too, can be found in a dual rainbow of styles and colors. Even gift tags come in an astonishing variety. For a minimum of investment, you can buy coordinated papers, ribbons, and gift cards. And you, too, can make the little gifts seem consequential and the important ones momentous.

Perhaps gift wrapping is one of life's littler pleasures, but don't underestimate its power to please. My grandmother taught me that. She had learned that, when the timing is right, even a trifling gift given for no reason at all can lift the spirits of a friend. Her routine was to go to Neiman-Marcus, a store renowned then (in the white-tissue era) for imaginative and beautiful gift wraps. She would buy a ladies' handkerchief or some other inexpensive present and have it gift wrapped in the distinctive Neiman-Marcus style.

She showed me that the beauty of a package, its unexpectedness, and—most important of all—the care involved in its preparation could lift the spirits of the recipient in a way quite out of proportion to the merit or value of the gift itself.

Wrapping packages perfectly—with just the right flair or touch—isn't hard, time-consuming, or even expensive. You don't have to invest more than a few dollars and you're not required to have the hand-eye coordination of a practiced surgeon. In the chapters that follow, you'll find that wrapping the basic box is easier than you think and that some of the most effective bows are the simplest to make. If you follow the step-by-step instructions, you'll also find that the more advanced techniques are surprisingly simple.

The easiest method of wrapping your own presents is to buy one roll of paper and a bag of prefabricated, stick-on bows. Chances are that that approach will succeed in obscuring the identity of the gift you're giving. On the other hand, giving a present is an occasion when you can reveal something of your care and affection, when you can demonstrate a mastery of certain skills, and even add a certain excitement to the occasion.

This little book will show you how. ≈ ≈ ≈

PART I

THE

RUDIMENTS

OF

WRAPPING

GETTING READY TO WRAP

*T*o tell you the truth, wrapping the perfect package isn't all that different from cooking an egg. It simply takes the right equipment, the appropriate materials, and, perhaps, a little practice. So before you set to work, let's get you set up.

THE EQUIPMENT

THE WORK SPACE

You need to have a surface on which to work. Unless you plan to wrap only small jewelry boxes, the space will have to be fairly large. Except in a pinch, then, your ironing board really isn't big enough. A tabletop is better.

SCISSORS

You will need scissors that are sharp and comfortable in your hand. You may also wish to have a pair of pinking shears to give a decorative crinkle-edged cut.

STICKY TAPE

The tape you use should be in a weighted, desk-style dispenser that allows you to reach and tear off pieces using only one hand. You can acquire such a dispenser for only a few dollars at most any store where stationery supplies are sold. The tape itself comes in a variety of styles. The most useful variety is clear, with a dull, matte finish that doesn't reflect light like glossy tape does. Matte-finish tape is the kind that seems to disappear when it is applied. Double-sided tape is good for attaching bows and gift cards and sealing certain kinds of packages invisibly. Colored tape can also be a good idea when you want to use the tape as part of your design.

MEASURING TAPE

A tailor's measuring tape is most useful for determining the amount of paper you will need for each package. This avoids having to guess how much paper is required—and all too often finding you have cut the sheet an inch too short—or rolling a box around on the paper (thus risking extra creases in the paper). By measuring carefully, you can make an accurate judgment of how much paper you will need and what shape it should be.

THE WRAPPING PAPER

As with any craft, gift wrapping requires raw materials. The greater the variety you have, of course, the wider variety of wraps you can make. But at the very least you require a simple paper and ribbon.

READY-MADE WRAPPING PAPER

The variety of wrapping papers available is staggering. There are patterns and colors and textures to suit every occasion and practically every taste.

Go to a well-stocked store and you will find papers that are whimsical and funny, sophisticated, and sentimental. They come in a range of weights and textures. Heavy and embossed papers are especially suitable for large packages, where the texture is shown to advantage and where the corners are not too small. Extra-heavy papers are good for making box-style wrappings. Lightweight papers can be used for all kinds of packages, especially those that are small or oddly shaped, since light papers are easy to fold.

For the purpose of your first few practice packages, however, you may want to go only as far as your newspaper pile.

OTHER WRAPPING-PAPER OPTIONS

Don't forget that both wallpaper and fabric can produce strikingly different and attractive packages.

Wallpaper is stiff and therefore most useful for wraps that need a crisp finish. You can even create a box (see the Petal Box on page 30) from it. Fabric is especially useful for awkward-sized gifts, as it can be draped around and gathered into a bundle.

With either fabric or wallpaper, the finished appearance of the package will be determined by the design on the material. Formal fabrics such as damask or silk will give a more formal look. Homespun fabrics such as calico or gingham are naturally informal. The same goes for wallpaper.

A formal paper produces a formal package, a folksy one a more relaxed appearance.

Still other possibilities include transparent wrappings such as Mylar and cellophane. For years these were consigned to wrapping baskets of fruit and Easter assemblages, but these plastic wrappings have recently come into their own, particularly when paired with tissue paper, lace, or other decorative material.

Mylar, a thin plastic, often looks opaque and metallic. It is characterized by its high sheen and strength. Unlike most wrapping materials, it is two-sided and you can retape it without its tearing.

Clear or tinted cellophane is also useful for its strength and sheen, particularly when wrapping oddly shaped packages. It can be retaped as well.

MAKING YOUR OWN PAPERS

You can also try making charming, personalized papers yourself. It's surprisingly easy. Using plain white tissue or shelf-liner paper, you can make a wrapping uniquely your own using watercolors, paints, felt-tip pens, crayons, decals, or stickers.

Another approach is to use stamps to decorate your homemade paper. Rubber stamps are available in a wide variety of shapes from crafts stores, and you can also make your own. A favorite arts-and-crafts activity for youngsters as early as preschool is that of making carved vegetable stamps. Potatoes, turnips, or carrots can be cut in half and a design carefully carved into the vegetable. They are then used with ink or paint to stamp designs.

Such papers can be great fun to make, and may provide an enjoyable rainy-day activity for your children. You can tailor such papers to fit the recipient's special interests or feature themes of the season or the event. Holiday designs such as Christmas trees, stars, and hearts are popular. Special-interest designs can include footballs or baseballs for the sports enthusiast, fish for the avid fisherman, or a spoon for the cook.

The easiest method for making paper is to create an all-over design on a sheet of paper. Remember, however, that you may need to allow time for the ink or paint to dry. When it's ready to use, you just cut and wrap as usual.

You may elect to create slightly more elaborate wrapping, perhaps by planning the design around the shape of the package to be wrapped. One way of doing this is by creating the design first and then wrapping the gift. You may find it useful to wrap the package once with scrap paper, and then use the first wrapper as a pattern for the final paper.

Another simple method, most suitable when using crayons, markers, stamps, or decals, is to wrap the package in white or other plain paper and create the design on the finished box *after* it's been wrapped.

Perhaps the only rule with wrapping paper is: *Don't be afraid to experiment.* If you can fold and tape it and it's safe to use, you might just put it to good use.

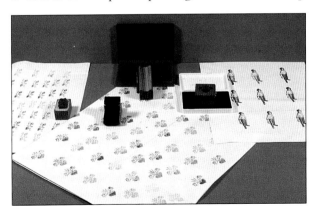

THE RIBBON

Traditionally, the well-wrapped package consists of a suitable combination of ribbon and paper. In many cases the ribbon can draw the eye, standing out in contrast to a simple paper. Ribbons can heighten the effect of a dominant color. But it is most often the bow—small or large, delicate or wildly splayed—that makes the splashiest statement.

Ribbons come in a wide variety of styles and sizes. They range from narrow to wide, and are available in various textures and shapes. Stationery stores carry a selection of styles specifically geared for package wrapping. The most common is satin. Most of these brands are self-adhesive when moistened and come in different widths. Other common varieties include curling ribbon, which is narrow and crinkled; and woven, which also comes in several widths. You may also find velvet-type ribbon in a variety of widths.

You need not be limited by wrapping ribbons from the stationery store, however. Ribbons made for sewing purposes, found at fabric stores, are elegant and beautiful when used on packages. Sewing ribbons are more expensive, but for a special package, nothing says you made an effort like a real velvet, satin, taffeta, piqué, or grosgrain ribbon. Such ribbons drape easily, making the wrapping task simple, and often look best with simple bows. With the right ribbon, you can use the simplest of papers and bows and yet achieve the maximum effect.

Other materials to use for ribbon include yarn, twine, string, raffia, and even thread. All of these materials come in a variety of colors and weights.

SOME FINISHING FLOURISHES

While bows on packages tend to take center stage, other flourishes, such as flowers—fresh, dried, pressed, or silk—or small toys, beads, candies, and pieces of costume jewelry can customize a package. An added gewgaw can make your gift stand out amidst a horde of others.

Sometimes such flourishes serve as the visual focus of the package, and a bow, if one is used, remains very simple. The Valentine package on page 51 is a good example. The focus of the present is a heart-shaped doily pierced with a Cupid gift card, set off by a simple lace bow. The Posted Wedding Gift on page 63 is another example of how a flourish is the decoration, in this case dried flowers nestled among simple ribbons. At other times a flourish and a bow work together to create an inviting centerpiece on the package. The Christmas present on page 48, which uses a Christmas tree ornament, and the Baby Present on page 72, which uses diaper pin decorations, are good examples of a fancy bow used with a special flourish.

WRAPPING GIFTS FOR SHIPPING

It's a good idea to avoid fluffy or elaborate bows when posting a package, as they all too frequently become crushed. Try to rely on plain flat bows such as the Simple Loop (see page 37) or a flattened Tailored Bow (see page 38).

Certain flourishes, including paper doilies, pressed flowers, candies, and pieces of colorful costume jewelry, can be shipped on a package more successfully than a delicate bow. When they arrive at their destination intact, they will deliver their original visual impact.

The Posted Wedding Gift on page 63 is a good example of how an effective flat presentation can be made. Such a package can be enclosed in a sturdy box or wrapped in shipping paper and sent as is, without further packaging. The same is true of a package using a doily or other paper cutout in an imaginative manner. If using candies or bits of costume jewelry, attach them securely before cushioning the gift in a box or padded shipping bag.

However you wrap your gift, make sure you wrap the box for shipping securely. Delicate presents should be padded in an extra box before wrapping with heavy brown paper. Be sure to seal the ends well with sturdy tape such as Mylar or reinforced packing tape. Address the package clearly. If using a marker that can run if it gets wet, cover the address and return address with clear tape. ≈ ≈ ≈

~ 2 ~

THE BASIC BOX

*Y*ou have selected your materials and set up your work space. Now it's time to wrap the basic box.

The methods for wrapping a symmetrically shaped package, be it a box, block, or book, are quite simple. There are two different ways you can fold the ends. Both methods work well for all boxes, so the choice is largely a matter of personal preference. You may find, however, depending on the size of the box and the way the paper you are using folds, that one method seems easier than the other.

WRAPPING THE BODY OF THE BOX

1. Measure the size of the box with a tailor's tape measure. Add an inch or two to the dimensions to allow for a fold for overlap and to hide the raw edges beneath.

2. Cut the paper to fit the box.

3. Place the box, top down, in the center of the paper. Fold over about half an inch of one long outside edge.

4. Pull the paper around the package, keeping the folded edge exposed. Align the straight ends of the package or, if the paper is patterned, align the patterns at the joint. Seal the folded edge with a piece of tape. If you wish, you may also tack down the inside edge, using a small piece of tape.

END FOLDING: METHOD 1

1. On each end of the package, press the paper in from the sides to form a pair of flaps, one

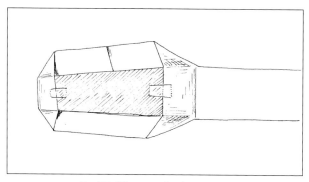

End Folding: Method 1, Step 1

on top and one on the bottom. Flatten the folds, creasing the edges with your fingers pinched together.

2. Fold down the top flap, which should be the one with the seam. Again, crease the fold to make a crisp edge.

3. Fold the raw edge of the remaining flap in to make a neat straight edge, then bring the folded edge up tautly to cover the first flap. Secure the edge with tape. If the edge is long, you may need several pieces of tape to secure it neatly.

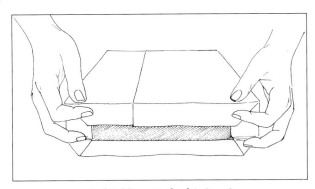

End Folding: Method 1, Step 2

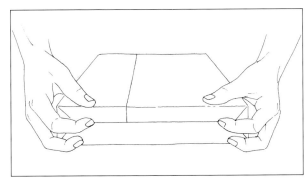

End Folding: Method 1, Step 3

4. Repeat the procedure with the paper at the other end of the package.

END FOLDING: METHOD 2

1. On each end of the package, fold the top edge of the paper down. Crease the top edge with your first and second fingers to make a crisp fold.

2. Fold in the end flaps toward the center. Be sure your folds are all crisp and flat.

3. Fold up the raw edge of the remaining flap to make a neat straight edge, then bring the folded edge up tautly to cover the first flap.

4. Repeat the steps for the opposite end of the package.

To give your package an all-over neat and crisp appearance, press your thumb and first finger together and run them around each edge.

3

WRAPPING THE ODDLY SHAPED PACKAGE

*N*ot everything fits into a neat box. Some of the best presents, in fact, are inconveniently asymmetrical and a challenge to the gift-wrapper. Have no fear: There are proven methods for wrapping such eccentric shapes. Below are techniques for wrapping bundles, bottles, jars, and cylinders. There's also one striking package—the Petal Box—that almost never fails to please.

You will find that tissue and thin papers are the easiest to handle in wrapping the oddball package. Given the nature of the material, however, it's usually a good idea to wrap the package in several thicknesses of paper. This will cushion the contents and help disguise its identity.

THE BUNDLE

Perhaps the simplest method for wrapping the unusually shaped gift is to turn it into a bundle. It works for a bean bag, a pair of sunglasses, a handful of bottle caps—for almost anything.

1. Measure the bundle with a tailor's tape measure to get the basic dimensions.

2. Cut a square of paper one and one-half times the measured dimensions of the bundle.

3. If you are using tissue paper, cut several pieces the same size. Place them one on top of another, and rotate them so that the corners do not overlap and a circle is formed.

4. Cut one (or even several) piece(s) of ribbon to a generous length, depending on the size of the package.

5. Place the package in the center of the paper and fold up the edges around it.

6. Tie the paper at the neck of the package with the ribbon, using a Basic Bow (see page 35). If you have several pieces of ribbon, tie them as one and then fan out the loops.

7. If you are using curling ribbon, curl the flowing ends (see page 36).

THE BOTTLE

The standard method for wrapping a bottle, particularly one containing liquid, is to wrap it as a cylinder with a gathered bundle-style top. The method is simple.

1. Measure the circumference and height of the bottle with a tailor's tape. Add two inches to the circumference for folding the edge and overlapping. Cut the paper to one and one-half times the bottle's height.

2. Cut one or several generous lengths of ribbon.

3. Fold one long edge of paper. If you wish to make a decorative top, cut the top edge of the paper in a scallop design.

4. Place the bottle on its side with enough room at the bottom end for the edges to be folded in under the bottle.

5. Roll the bottle in the paper and secure the folded edge with tape or a sticker.

6. Fold in the bottom using one of the two methods for folding ends (see pages 24–25) or by making a series of small folds toward the center. Secure the last fold with tape or a round sticker.

7. Gather the top with a length of ribbon, as in the bundle method.

THE JAR

Jars may be wrapped the same way as bottles, though the top can also be sealed in the same manner as the bottom using tape or a sticker. A ribbon may then be tied around the neck of the jar or a bow stuck on the top.

A Fluffy Bow (see page 39) placed on top makes a stunning presentation. For a casual look, try wrapping a jar of homemade pickles or jam using a piece of fabric such as calico or gingham, as you would for a bottle. Tie with a flowing ribbon into a Basic Bow (see page 35).

THE CYLINDER

For many irregularly shaped packages, bundles are an easy and attractive method of wrapping. However, for a formal present or event (or when you don't want people guessing what it is because of its shape), sometimes a satisfactory option is to make an irregularly shaped package more regular.

One method for regularizing a package's shape is particularly well suited to objects that are essentially long and thin, or ones that can be made so.

1. Wrap the object in tissue or other paper to cushion it.

2. Cut a piece of flexible corrugated cardboard to a size that fits comfortably around the object. If the object is fragile, you might make it larger in diameter and fill the resulting tube with extra cushioning paper.

3. Wrap the cardboard around the object, and secure the seam with tape or a sticker.

4. Stuff the ends with tissue or other paper.

5. Follow the basic procedure for wrapping a bottle or jar. Before cutting the paper, decide what kind of ends you would like. You may leave both ends long and tie them to look like a party popper, or make them more tailored by folding them in and sealing with stickers.

THE PETAL BOX

This eye-catching wrap looks as though it is difficult to make. But don't be fooled—it isn't.

The Petal Box is essentially a Japanese origami paper box. Its delicate look makes it particularly appropriate for small packages.

1. Measure the overall width and height of your package.

2. Draw a circle on heavy wrapping paper roughly three times the size of the largest dimension of your package and cut it out. If, for example, you are wrapping a three-inch-round

The Cylinder

ornament, you would draw a nine-inch circle. A five-inch-high, three-inch-wide vase would require a fifteen-inch circle.

3. Place an object with a circular bottom, such as a glass, slightly larger than the diameter of your package in the center of the paper. Thus, continuing to use the above examples, both the ornament and the vase would require about a three-and-one-half-inch circle. Fold the paper up around the object to form a circular crease. Remove the object.

4. On what is to be the inside of the package, lightly draw lines that divide the circle into eight equal segments. Fold the paper along the lines of the segments from the edge to the creased circle.

5. On either side of each line, punch a hole (there should be sixteen holes in total).

6. Run a ribbon or cord through the holes.

7. Wrap the object in a bit of tissue or other paper, and place in the center of the package.

8. Pull the ribbons to form a petal-shaped box, and tie them into a Basic Bow (see page 35).

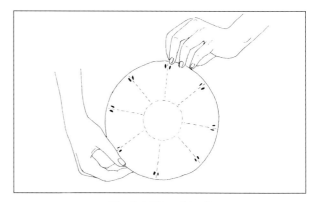

The Petal Box, Step 5

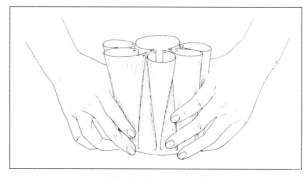

The Petal Box, Step 6

4

FIVE BASIC BOWS

For many a package, the bow is the centerpiece. In the case of the lazy package-wrapper, that means a commercial bow of the peel-and-stick variety has been added. However, with just a tiny bit more effort, you can make much more satisfactory bows.

Your own creations can be as simple as the bow you use to tie your shoes, but made elegant with a beautiful ribbon. They can be tailored and simple, or flamboyantly frilly. Either way, they'll add a special touch to any gift.

Five examples of the most useful gift-wrapping bows follow, along with basic advice on applying the ribbon to the package. The first bow, the Most Basic Bow, can be made from the same piece of ribbon you use for wrapping the package. All the others are attached separately. There are two methods of tying ribbons and a note on curling ribbons. The directions in each case are given for right-handed people, so you should reverse them if you are left-handed.

BASIC RIBBON TYING

Before adding the bow that will complete your gift, you may want to tie a ribbon around the entire package. Your bow may be made directly with this ribbon or you may seal the ends of the wrapping ribbon to the package and attach the bow to it.

There are two basic methods for wrapping a package with a ribbon. The first uses all four corners of the box, the second uses two.

1. Measure the distance around the box both the long way and around the waist. Add a few inches to the total of the two and cut a piece of ribbon to the resulting length. If you plan to tie the bow with the same piece of ribbon, you must add sufficient ribbon for that as well. You can also approximate by taking a generous amount of ribbon and waiting until the ribbon is tied before cutting it from the roll.

2. Place the middle of the ribbon's length in the center of the front of the package.

3. Flipping the box, bring the two ends of the ribbon to the back of the package. Cross the ribbons and extend the ends perpendicular to the loop already around the box.

4. Flip the box again (onto its back), and bring the ribbon back to the starting point in front. Tie or seal the ends with tape or moisture if using self-stick satin ribbon.

≈

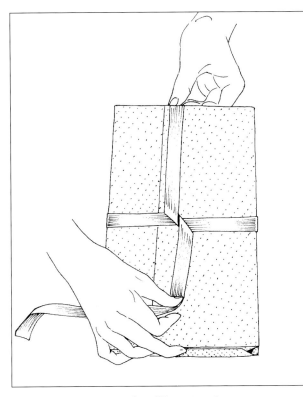

Tying the Ribbon, Step 3

TYING A DIAGONAL RIBBON

1. Measure the box using a tailor's tape from one corner to the diagonal corner and around the back to the first corner. Double the measurement for the ribbon. Add an inch or two if attaching a bow or a good deal more if you plan to tie a bow directly.

2. Place the middle of the length of ribbon on the front of the corner of your choice. Bring the ribbon around the corner and diagonally across the back of the package to the opposite corner.

3. Bring the ends of the ribbon to the front of the package and tie or seal with tape or moisture if using self-stick satin ribbon.

THE MOST BASIC BOW

This bow is the one that we all were taught when learning to tie our shoes. As basic as it is, this bow looks wonderful, especially when made with good-quality woven ribbons such as grosgrain, satin, taffeta, velvet, and moiré, particularly the soft kinds used for sewing. It is also the principal bow for curling ribbon.

Such ribbons come in an endless array of colors, widths, styles, and patterns. Gift-wrapping ribbons of all kinds are also used for the Basic Bow; in general, the narrower and softer types, such as crinkled curling ribbons and Mylar ribbons, achieve the best effects, particularly when used in multiples. The Basic Bow is usually tied as part of the ribbon encircling a package, but it can also be attached separately, as described here.

1. Take a length of ribbon and form a loop in your left hand, holding the point of crossing with your thumb and forefinger.

2. Bring the remaining end around your pinched fingers.

3. Push your other index finger into the free ribbon to form a loop. Pass the loop through the second small loop.

4. Free your fingers and tighten the two big loops, leaving the ends dangling.

5. Attach a small piece of double-sided tape or a loop of single-sided tape to the back of the bow and press into place on the package.

CURLING RIBBON

A wonderful addition to the Basic Bow is to finish up the ends with curling ribbon. Almost everyone seems familiar with curling ribbon. For many, the only way to finish a package is to add that curl to the ribbons. Creating the flowing tendrils that fall gracefully over a package, however, is not as easy as it seems—all too often the ribbon flattens out or doesn't curl enough.

Try it this way. Take a piece of ribbon in your left hand and a pair of scissors in your right. Position one end of the ribbon on a blade of the scissors, turned slightly on the diagonal. Place your right thumb gently but firmly over the ribbon and pull the ribbon over the blade. The more pressure you apply, the tighter the curl.

THE SIMPLE LOOP

This ribbon treatment is even simpler than the Basic Bow and very effective when you desire a reserved and dignified look.

The Simple Loop can be made in any size and with a wide variety of ribbons, including woven and nonwoven. You can use it singly or two or three together in graduated sizes. The tails can be long or short, and the loop large or small. The directions here are given for a bow using nine inches of $1^{3}/_{16}$-inch ribbon, which makes a four-inch bow.

1. Hold the length of ribbon near the ends.

2. Move your hands together and cross the ribbons, right over left or left over right.

3. Adjust the loop and tails as you wish. Secure the ribbon at the crossing with a piece of tape; if using self-stick ribbon, simply moisten the overlapping piece of ribbon in back.

4. Fold the end of the ribbons in half along the ribbon's length. Then make an angled cut to

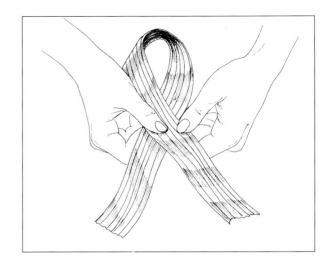

produce an inverted **V** at the ribbon ends.

5. Attach a small piece of double-sided tape or a loop of single-sided tape to the back of the bow and attach to the package. If using self-stick ribbon for both tying ribbon and bow, moisten the back and press onto the package over the tied ribbon.

THE TAILORED BOW

The Tailored Bow looks neat and sophisticated on a package. You can keep it plain and simple with but two loops, or make it more elaborate by adding more pairs of loops.

Tailored Bows are easily made from almost any kind of dressmaker's or gift ribbon, though stiffer ribbons seem to produce the best results. Tailored Bows are also suitable for a wide variety of widths—from narrow curling ribbon, best used for a very small bow, up to ribbons of two or more inches in width. Nonwoven satin gift ribbon is particularly well-suited to this treatment.

The bow shown here is about six inches wide, with a pair of loops on each side and a circle at the top, and uses a $1^3/_{16}$-inch-wide ribbon.

1. Cut a piece of ribbon about a yard long.

2. Form a loop, bringing the ribbon in front, about six inches from the end. Pinch the joint with your left hand.

3. Form another loop, a mirror image of the first, and pinch the third layer of ribbon with your left hand.

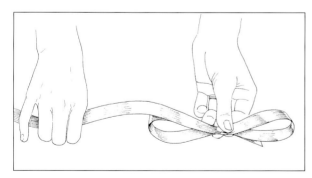

The Tailored Bow, Step 3

The Tailored Bow, Step 5

4. Form a third, slightly smaller loop atop the first; now a fourth, atop the second.

5. Bring the ribbon tail around into a circular loop in the center.

6. Secure the bow in the center with a small piece of tape wrapped through the final loop and around the remaining layers. If using self-stick ribbon, moisten the center of each layer as you fold and moisten the end before folding into the final loop.

7. Attach a small piece of double-sided tape or a loop of single-sided tape to the back of the bow and attach to the package. If using self-stick ribbon for both tying ribbon and bow, moisten the back and press onto the package over the tied ribbon.

THE FLUFFY BOW

This bow looks quite festive and celebratory. You may think it's hard to make, but, like the rest, there's no great mystery.

A Fluffy Bow can be made with a variety of ribbons. Stiff ribbons will give a crisp, sophisticated, and formal look, while softer ones offer a more flowing and casual look. Overall, crisp ribbons such as taffeta, moiré, piqué, and non-woven satin ribbons (the kind most often found in stationery or party stores) are easiest to manipulate. Wide ribbons make the fullest bows.

In addition to the primary ribbon, you will also need a piece of narrow ribbon or string to secure the center. You may use a piece of the same ribbon folded or split, or another narrower ribbon. This bow uses quite a lot of ribbon.

1. For a bow about six inches across, you will need a bit more than a yard of ribbon. To figure the amount for a different size, decide the diameter you wish, then multiply by the number of loops you wish and add a few inches for the tails. While six loops are usual, you can use eight or ten. This bow, for example, is made of six six-inch loops and requires about forty inches; one of eight six-inch loops would require a bit more than fifty, and so on.

2. Starting a few inches from the end of the ribbon, make a three-inch-long loop and pinch the base with your thumb and index finger.

3. With your free hand, form another loop opposite the first and pinch it in at the center along with the first loop.

4. Repeat the procedure four more times, alternating sides, always holding the center of the bow. You will end up with three loops on each side of the bow. The number of loops is infinitely variable; in general, the more loops, the fluffier the bow, the fewer loops, the more tailored the look.

5. Tie the center of the bow with a small piece of ribbon or string, or secure it by twisting a wire tie around it. Fluff out the loops as needed. Trim the tails by folding the end of the ribbons in half along the ribbon's length. Then make an angled cut to produce an inverted V at the ribbon ends.

6. Attach to the package by one of two methods. If the package is tied with a ribbon, tie the bow on using a thin piece of ribbon. If no ribbon

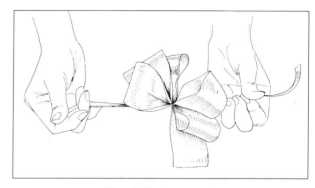

The Fluffy Bow, Step 5

has been tied, attach the bow using a small piece of double-sided tape or a loop of single-sided tape.

THE BLOSSOM BOW

This decoration is not technically a bow since it is neither knotted nor made from ribbon or string, but it still stands in as one since in makes a spectacular decorative addition to a package.

The Blossom Bow can be made from any soft or pliable paper such as tissue paper, crepe paper, cellophane, or Mylar, and it looks particularly good when made with patterned paper or with alternating colors for the layers. The directions given are for a bow about six inches in diameter, but it can be made to almost any size.

1. Cut out six or eight circles of paper about seven inches in diameter. The easiest method is to fold a single sheet into six or eight portions and cut once.

2. Cut a piece of narrow ribbon, large enough to wrap around the package, or short enough to tie the base of the bow if the Blossom Bow is to be stuck on the gift separately.

3. Gather the circles of paper in your left hand. Press your right index finger into the center of the circles.

4. Press a dime into the base of the "stem" you have just shaped with your finger, and tie the stem about an inch from the base, using the ribbon. A rubber band or a wire twist-tie may also be used to bunch the base of the Blossom Bow.

5. Fluff out the layers of the blossom to form ruffled petals.

6. To attach to the package, flatten the bottom of the bow and attach pieces of double-sided tape or a loop of single-sided tape and place on the package.

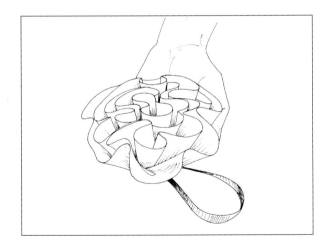

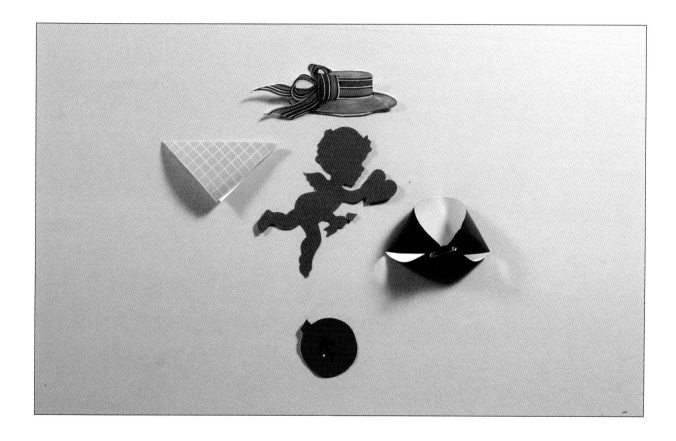

5

THE GIFT CARD

*I*t's a romantic evening for just the two of you. You slide a beautifully wrapped package for your loved one over the linen tablecloth. Amidst candle-glow and soft music, it's obvious that the most important person in the world is sitting right there, only a gaze away.

That package may not need a gift card, but in any circumstance in which there are more than two people involved, the giver of the gift or even the recipient may not be as obvious.

Gift tags and cards are usually small so that they don't overwhelm a package. A selection of such labels is generally available in a wide variety of styles, ranging from inexpensive stick-ons to tiny cards complete with envelopes that are to be hung from the ribbon. Merchandise tags found in stationery or office-supply stores also make good gift tags, as they usually come with string to be tied on to a ribbon. Another good option, especially if you have a message to add to your gift, is a greeting card attached to your gift.

You may, however, want to create your own unique homemade gift tag. It can be as simple as a small piece of the wrapping paper so it coordinates with your package. Geometric shapes—triangles, squares, even little curves—are easy to cut. Fold a small piece of paper, and cut whatever shape you wish, making sure you don't cut off all the fold. Then write your message on the inside and attach to the package, using tape or a decorative seal.

A slightly different effect can be achieved by cutting a shape from a single sheet of heavy paper or card stock. If using patterned paper, write your message on the blank side before attaching it with a small piece of double-sided tape or a sticker, or by punching a small hole for a ribbon in order to tie the label to the package.

Where do you place the tag? No hard-and-fast rules apply here, as gift tags can be placed anywhere on a package. When they are particularly pretty, clever, elaborate, or are used instead of a ribbon decoration, however, they should take prominence and be placed in the center or near a corner. On other hand, when they are minor decorative elements used in conjunction with other decorations such as ribbons and bows, tags should be placed more discreetly. They can peek out from under a bow or section of the ribbon.

Just remember that wherever you place a tag, it should not be so discreet that the recipient will fail to see it. ≈ ≈ ≈

PART II

GREAT GIFT WRAPPING FOR ALL OCCASIONS

~ 6 ~

HOLIDAYS

*O*ne thing about a beautifully wrapped present—it's always a joy to give. Now that you are familiar with a few of the basic methods for wrapping packages and making bows, we will take a look at a few ideas for creating packages for special occasions.

Keep in mind that many of the treatments shown in the following pages are interchangeable with one another. They can also be altered slightly to suit a different event. You can mix-and-match at your whim and to suit your taste: Try a different bow, a change of paper, or another tag, and you'll create a whole new look.

The Christmas season is demanding in many ways—not least because of the sheer number of packages to be wrapped before December 25th. Some of us find ourselves up until three o'clock in the morning every Christmas Eve, vowing never to be caught short again.

The trick to avoiding such last-minute madness is, of course, not to leave it all until Santa's step is heard up on the roof. If you can start at least a week ahead and wrap a few packages a day, you will not only get a good night's sleep on Christmas Eve, you will enjoy the wrapping process much more.

This elegant package makes use of rich-looking paper, a luxurious ribbon, and the added fillip of a Christmas ornament.

Try using a colorful satin cord or a fairly stiff ribbon. Wrap it diagonally around the box at the corners, securing the ends at the front with tape (see page 35).

Make a Fluffy Bow from the same cord or ribbon (see page 39). Secure it with a piece of narrow curling ribbon in a matching or coordinating color. Tie the bow to the box ribbon (over the meeting ends), and tie an ornament on using the curling ribbon.

Other fairly stiff ribbons such as woven grosgrain, taffeta, or moiré work well, too. A sprig of fresh holly or other evergreen or a pretty gift tag could be used in place of an ornament.

This rectangular package has a festive feel. Several simple elements are combined here to achieve the effect. The Blossom Bow almost looks like a Christmas decoration on its own, especially on the backdrop of the shiny paper.

To make this design, wrap a piece of ribbon around the wrapped box, crossing the pieces in the back (see page 34). Secure the ends on top with tape (if using self-stick ribbon, moisten the ends and press together to seal).

Many kinds of ribbon can be used to wrap the box. You might try using a plain paper ribbon in a color coordinated to the bow (such as green if the bow is red). Several pieces of curling ribbon adds a sprightly touch. Whatever ribbon you choose, your best choice is almost always to keep it fairly simple—you want the fluffy decoration to garner most of the attention.

Make a Blossom Bow (see page 40) using Mylar, a plastic paper with a metallic sheen (as shown), or tissue paper. The paper you use can match the ribbon or coordinate with another color in the wrapping paper. Secure the bow with a long piece of curling ribbon. Curl the ribbon ends (see page 36). Attach to the box over the sealed ribbon ends with a piece of double-sided tape or a loop of single-sided tape.

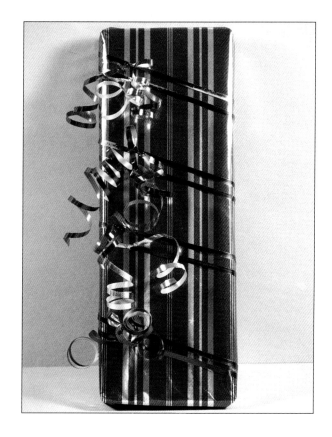

The asymmetrical ribbon treatment on this package is appropriate for almost any occasion, be it Christmas or Hanukkah, Father's Day or a wedding anniversary. The key is that the present be wrapped in a long rectangular box.

To make this package, wrap the box in a simple paper. Next, secure the ends of three narrow curling ribbons in the back at the top left corner. Holding the ribbons in one hand, bring them around to the front and across the package diagonally, around the back diagonally, and around the front diagonally again. Continue to work down the package until you reach the lower right corner. Secure the ribbons in back with a small piece of tape.

Cut eight to twelve lengths of curling ribbon, each about a foot long, and tie them to bands of ribbons as they appear on the left side. Curl each ribbon gently (see page 36). To make a row of bows, descending the side, cut the ribbons a few inches longer and tie into Basic Bows (see page 35) before curling the ends.

Valentine's Day is a day for sentiment and, as kids say, "mushy stuff." So why not go all out with feminine hearts and lace?

For this wrap we've used a plain paper that shows off its pretty lace, ribbon, and the decorative paper doily. After wrapping the box (see page 24), cut equal lengths of wide lace and of woven ribbon. Then wrap both the lace (on top) and the ribbon diagonally around the corners of the box. Tie the combined ends of the lace and ribbon in the top left corner, leaving the ends hanging. You'll need them.

Using lengths of about a yard each of combined lace and ribbon, make a Fluffy Bow (see page 39), without securing the center. Lay the bow on the package in the top left corner. Take about a foot of lace, loop it under the double-wrapped lace at the center, of the bow, bring it around the center and tie with a Basic Bow (see page 35).

To make the decoration and gift tag, cut the center from a heart-shaped doily and attach it to the package using double-sided tape. This Cupid, to be found at stationery or party stores or cut from a piece of heavy paper if you have the artistic touch, serves as a gift tag. Just position his legs inside the cut-out heart to hold him in place.

A different effect can be achieved by wrapping wide lace once around the corners. The wider lace makes for a luxurious bow, too.

≈

Mother's Day evokes a rosy image of breakfast in bed, a day of leisure, a nice card, and a thoughtful present. There's room in the picture for thoughtful wrapping, too.

This package coordinates the paper and decoration, using a paper with a fleur-de-lis design and small bouquet of dried flowers. The bouquet is simply tucked under the Basic Bow (see page 35). The soft woven ribbon drapes easily, and the ensemble result is elegant and feminine.

A small bouquet of fresh flowers—or a single stem—slipped in just before the presentation would give a smashing look, too.

As another option, you can make a children's project of wrapping Mom's special present—it can be fun and rewarding. Start by making the paper, as discussed on page 18. Crayons, markers, rubber stamps, even customized shapes cut from potatoes (potato stamps) are all good materials to use. Once the paper is made, the package can be wrapped as a box (see page 24) or a bundle (see page 28) and tied with a simple ribbon and bow.

A traditional Father's Day gift (how about a nice striped shirt and coordinating tie?) provides a good opportunity to make a dignified and classic presentation.

This simple wrap is made elegant by the use of first-rate materials— the key is the beautiful ribbon. Shown here is a woven striped taffeta ribbon, a kind to be found in a fabric store. A ribbon with a pattern gives the package interest; stripes, polka dots, and floral patterns are just some of those available. Moiré, taffeta, and grosgrain all work as well.

To take best advantage of the handsome ribbon, wrap the package in a plain-colored paper. Use a good-quality heavy paper, if possible. You could also use a piece of wallpaper with an embossed pattern, or a fabric such as damask or jacquard. Take a length of good-quality ribbon (about two yards for a shirt box), and wrap it diagonally around the corners and tie into a Basic Bow (see page 35).

Make a simple gift card from a piece of wrapping paper, and attach in one corner using double-sided tape.

~ 7 ~

BIRTHDAYS

*W*ho doesn't remember as a child wondering how you could possibly wait a whole *year* until your next birthday? For many people, some part deep down in us retains that childlike wishfulness all our lives.

A birthday is special: The event belongs to that person and no one else. That's why we celebrate them. Sometimes the celebration is public and loud and raucous; at other times, the manner is more muted. But the day should *always* be acknowledged.

A CHILD'S BIRTHDAY

When it comes to children, the day is almost guaranteed to be one of great energy, with high spirits and loud excitement in full display. The package here, dripping with its springy curls, echoes such feelings.

Wrap a box with a bright and exciting paper. Tissue paper, as shown here, is easy for a youngster to tear off. Cut several curling ribbons of differing but generous lengths, widths, and colors. Hold them together and wrap around the box, crossing the ribbons in back (see page 34). Tie into a Basic Bow (see page 35), and fan out the loops.

Take several more ribbons, hold together, loop under the bow, and tie into another Basic Bow. Fan out the loops. Curl the ends by pulling each ribbon against the blade of a pair of scissors (see page 36).

If you want a less full bow, omit the second set of ribbons. With a slightly smaller bow, you can enhance the package with a flourish by adding a piece or two of wrapped candy or a small, inexpensive toy. Tie it to the bow or attach to the package with tape.

THE LADY'S BIRTHDAY

This simple but effective presentation is suitable for a variety of occasions, but the delicate, feminine print of the paper makes it especially appropriate for a girl's or woman's birthday. The secret to the success of this package is in the ribbon: A soft woven satin picot-edged ribbon, which you'll find in crafts or fabric stores, allows the loose bow to drape gracefully. To make this package, wrap a box in pretty paper with a small print. Tie the ribbon around the box, crossing the ends in the back (see page 34) before bringing the ribbon to the front and crossing it there.

Use ribbon in a coordinating or matching color. Cut a piece about eighteen inches long, and loop it around your hand twice. Remove from your hand, pinch in the middle, and place in the center

of the crossed ribbon on the box. Bring the loose ends of the box ribbon up around the loops and tie into a Basic Bow (see page 35).

A GIFT FOR HIM

Here's a perfect wrap for the classic man's birthday present, the tie. In this case, the pattern on the simple, heavy paper was selected because it echoes the paisley design of the tie. There's a self-stick satin ribbon on this one, but any fairly crisp ribbon such as taffeta, moiré, or grosgrain will work well. The ribbon should be stiff enough to hold the shape of the loops when folded.

Tie the ribbon around the box, crossing in back (see page 34). Bring the ends together slightly above the center and tape rather than tie them. Make a slightly oversized Tailored Bow, described on page 38, and place it over the sealed ends. Attach with a piece of double-sided tape, or, if using self-stick ribbon, by moistening the bottom of the bow and pressing it down.

A simple gift tag cut to match a design element from the paper (in this case a paisley shape) or a geometric shape and placed unobtrusively in a corner or under the bow will finish off the package.

AN ALL-PURPOSE PACKAGE

It's often difficult to know how best to show off a cylindrical package, whether it contains a perfume bottle, a cocktail glass, or a jar of caviar. One method is to use a Blossom Bow. The oversized blossom stands out above the smaller cylinder. With this kind of bow you also don't have to worry about getting a ribbon to stay on the rounded surface of the cylinder.

To make this package, wrap the cylinder as described on page 29. Make a Blossom Bow (see page 40) using tissue or crepe paper. Cut the strings short or leave long and curl before attaching to the package with tape.

~ 8 ~

WEDDINGS

*G*ifts abound in the sequence of events that culminates in a wedding. There are shower gifts to the bride and groom. There are bridesmaids' and groomsmen's presents, all given and received with high spirits and great joy. And then there are the wedding gifts.

THE WEDDING GIFT

Wedding packages are usually wrapped in the traditional wedding colors of white, silver, or gold, often with accents of light blue or pink. Patterns in paper tend to be simple. Today you often see colored wrappings as well, but they are usually in pastel colors.

The package shown here is a classic wrap updated, and is suitable for a wedding or a special anniversary such as a twenty-fifth. Instead of white or silver paper, a silver moiré-patterned Mylar is used here. The white moiré ribbon adds a crisp and formal look.

To do this one, tie the wrapped box with ribbon, crossing the ends in back (see page 34), knotting in front, and leaving tails three or four inches long. Make a Fluffy Bow (see page 39), tying it with cord or a small piece of very thin silver curling ribbon. Attach the bow to the center of the ribbon with the curling ribbon or cord.

THE POSTED WEDDING GIFT

No doubt at one time or another you've found yourself in the position of having to mail a wedding gift. Trying to create a pretty package that can withstand the rigors of the post can be a challenge. One solution is to make the design flat, so that you need not worry about crushing a bow.

This package relies on the combination of a simple ribbon and pressed flowers. The effect is a little like flowers growing from a trellis. If you don't have pressed flowers, a dramatic presentation can be made using flowers, wedding bells, or champagne glasses made of paper. These can be either bought or made.

To make this package, wrap the box in a simple heavy paper. Wrap a narrow ribbon lengthwise around the box twice, leaving a space between the ribbons. Seal the ribbon in back with tape. Slip the stems of several pressed flowers underneath the ribbon. The bachelor's buttons shown here seem especially appropriate. Secure each stem under the ribbon with a tiny piece of tape.

This wrap is good for either a bridal shower or a wedding present. If used for a wedding present, you might wish to use a white ribbon.

The distinctive element of this package is the spiral ribbon on top. It works best when made of a fairly crisp ribbon such as nonwoven satin, moiré, or taffeta so that it holds its shape.

To make this package, wrap the box in a simple plaid, stripe, or other pa-

per. Tie the ribbon, crossing the ends in the back (see page 34) and taping the ends to seal.

Next, take about eighteen inches of ribbon and fold one end in on itself to form a small circular loop. Pinch the base of the loop with two fingers to hold it. Wrap the ribbon around the first loop in a slightly larger circle. At the base of the loop, slip the ribbon between your pinched fingers to hold it. Continue looping the ribbon to form increasingly large circles, all the while pinching at the base to hold it. Secure the base of the bow with a piece of tape wrapped around all the layers.

Attach to the package with a piece of double-sided tape. To finish the package, pass a small piece of ribbon through the loop and seal on either side of the loop with double-sided tape.

INSTANT-OPENING FABRIC-WRAPPED PRESENT

Here's a wrap that is easy to dress up or down, stands out on a crowded table of gifts, and even comes through the mail well. (It's also good for the anxious bride or groom who can't wait to get into the package.) Instead of using paper, it's been wrapped with scrap fabric. No tape has been used since it doesn't stick well to fabric, and the ribbon is tied so that the ribbon unwraps easily by pulling the ends.

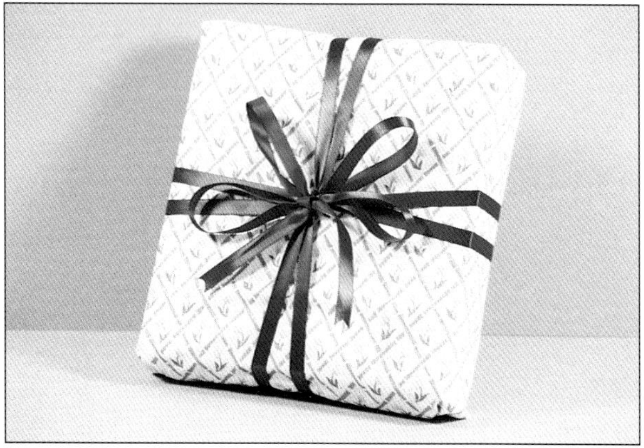

To make the package, wrap a box using fabric; an informal cotton chintz is shown here. For a less casual look, you might use a formal print such as a white-on-white pattern or damask. You may tape the ends to hold the fabric in place while you tie the ribbon. Use woven ribbon, such as satin, picot-edged satin, or grosgrain, which you'll find in a crafts or fabric store. Wrap the ribbon around the material twice, crossing in back (see page 34). Then tie into the Basic Bow (see page 35) in front, and using the extra long ends tie another Basic Bow. Once tied, remove the tape—it probably won't stick well anyway.

THE BRIDESMAID'S PRESENT

This feminine-looking package is perfect for a bridesmaid's gift. Its delicate scale comes from using very thin curling ribbon and a small-patterned paper. A tiny fresh blossom (preferably of wedding flowers) or a tiny sprig of dried flowers tucked under the bow further customizes the package.

Wrap a small package in a paper to coordinate with the colors of the wedding. Tie tiny curling ribbons around the box (see page 34), leaving plenty of extra ribbon for tying a Basic Bow (see page 35) and curling the ends.

Before making the bow, take a separate piece of ribbon and wrap around two or three fingers to make several loops, leaving short ends. Pinch the loops in the middle and place in the center of the package ribbon. Bring the long ends of ribbon around the loops and tie into a Basic Bow. Curl the ends into soft tendrils (see page 36). Tuck a small sprig of flowers or a blossom under the knot.

A GIFT FOR THE GROOMSMAN

This geometrically wrapped box suits a groomsman's gift, as well as gifts for numerous other occasions. The wrap can be plain or, as here, in a grid pattern. Simple ribbon, such as nonwoven satin, looks crisp.

The ribbons and bows look complex, but are quite simple to do. Measure the box and cut four ribbons just long enough to overlap. Wrap each one around the box and seal in front with a small piece of double-sided tape.

Now make two Tailored Bows (see page 38) and place over the ends of the crossed ribbons in the center of the box. Attach with double-sided tape or, if using self-stick ribbon, by moistening the bottom of each bow and pressing in place. To further accent the geometric qualities of the wrap, cut a gift tag of the same paper and attach it in one corner.

~ 9 ~

MILESTONES

One way we mark various stages of our lives is with milestone events, such as graduations, the births of babies, and job promotions or retirement. The giving of presents helps us acknowledge in a tangible way our joy at the arrival of such happy events. Each of these is especially well suited to the imaginatively wrapped gift.

Graduation, be it from high school, college, or graduate school, is a time for joyous celebration—and heaving a big sigh of relief over having cleared a major hurdle.

The small box shown here makes a point of the tangible result of graduation, the diploma, by using a mock diploma as a gift tag. It uses a paper with a pattern that is distinct but not so large or busy that it detracts from the main decoration. No other ribbon is needed.

Wrap a box as shown on page 24. Cut a rectangle of heavy paper in a plain but coordinating color. Write your message on the paper. Roll the paper, with the message on the inside, into a tube and pull one end of the paper out slightly. Tie the "diploma" with a Basic Bow (see page 35) of thin ribbon. You can also use curling, grosgrain, or satin ribbon. Secure to the package at a slight angle using double-sided tape or a loop of single-sided tape.

THE JOB PROMOTION

A big job promotion deserves recognition, even if it's a half-facetious gesture, such as giving a "power tie." This package uses very simple elements to achieve a customized look. Crisp ribbons such as nonwoven satin, grosgrain, moiré, or taffeta keep their shape best.

To make this package, start by measuring the box and cutting plain paper to fit (see page 24). Mark the corners of the top edge very lightly on the paper. Customize the paper using rubber stamps in a pattern that aligns with the top of the box. Wrap the box and tie with ribbon, crossing it in the back (see page 34) and sealing the ends in front. Make a Simple Loop (see page 37) and attach to the ribbon where the ends meet, using tape or, if using self-stick ribbon, by moistening the back of the bow.

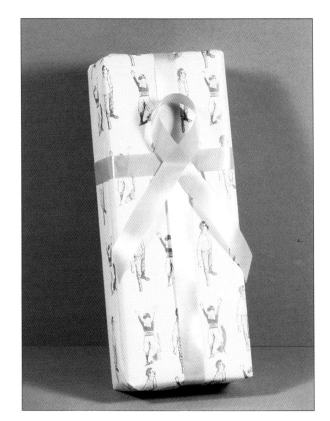

Baby presents often reflect the sense of giddy happiness that prevails at an impending arrival. Packages are usually wrapped in papers and ribbons predominantly pastel in color.

The wrap shown here uses several pieces of very thin curling ribbon in colors coordinated with the paper. After wrapping the box, wrap the ribbon diagonally around the corners (see page 35), leaving an extra two feet or so for the bow and curling.

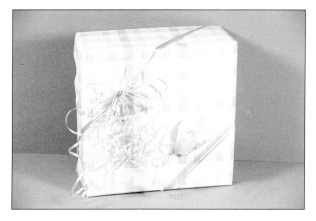

Before tying the Basic Bow, take another piece of ribbon and form several loops by wrapping it around two or three fingers. Pinch the loops in the center and place at the knot of the main ribbons. Bring the ends up and around the loops and tie the ends into a Basic Bow (see page 35). Curl the long ribbon ends (see page 36).

For an added flourish, you might want to thread a couple of toy diaper pins or a baby bracelet through the ribbon ends and tie.

One cute and useful flourish is to make a gift tag in the shape of a diaper. Take a triangle of paper, fold in the two side flaps, and then bring the bottom flap up. Secure with a tiny safety pin. Write your message on a small bit of paper and place in the "diaper."

We all know the cliché about good things coming in small packages. Yet sometimes it's hard to make a small package stand out. You want that perfect bijou to announce its importance with authority. It need not scream, but rather should be quietly elegant and perfectly proportioned.

Small packages often need a delicate touch. Paper patterns should be fairly small and ribbons scaled to suit the size. This asymmetrically wrapped package is simple yet elegant.

After wrapping the box in paper, tie the ribbon around the box, starting above the center. Cross the ribbons in back off to one side, and bring around to the front. Seal the ribbon over the crossed joint.

Now cut two lengths of ribbon, about seven inches long. One of the ribbons should be narrower in width and in a contrasting color. Place the narrower ribbon over the wider one and make a Simple Loop (page 37). Position the bow at the crossed joint, facing the upper left corner. Attach to the package using a small piece of double-sided tape or a loop of single-sided tape.

ENTERTAINING

*W*hen you go to visit friends in their new home, a housewarming gift can help express your congratulations. When you go for a stay, a hostess gift is a must—it doesn't have to be fancy, but it's an appropriate expression of thanks. Or perhaps *you're* having the party and you want to offer token party favors to your guests to make the occasion more memorable.

You might try wraps like those that follow for these occasions.

This festive bundle is simple to make (inside is a jar of tasty preserves). The key to making it look special is to use generous-sized pieces of paper to make it seem to explode from the ribbon. Tissue paper is shown here, but colored cellophane and Mylar work well, too. The other trick to making the package work visually is to be sure the paper doesn't get crushed during transport.

Wrap the package into a bundle, as shown on page 28. Take several generous-sized pieces of curling ribbon, gather the paper, and tie into a Basic Bow (see page 35). Curl the ends of the ribbon (see page 36).

THE HOSTESS GIFT

Taking a small offering such as a bottle of wine, olive oil, or fancy vinegar—to name only a few possibilities—to a dinner party is considered a polite gesture. Rather than just handing over a naked gift, you can make a pleasing statement with a simple wrap.

This treatment uses a bottle wrapped in tissue paper. Follow the directions for wrapping a bottle on page 28, leaving the top open and making deep slashes in the paper about every half inch. Cut a length of soft ribbon, about eighteen inches long—here we've used woven satin picot-edge. Gather the top paper with the ribbon and tie into a Basic Bow (see page 35). Attach a gift card with a string, if you wish. Carefully and gently curl the slashed pieces of tissue paper (see page 36).

A PARTY FAVOR

Party favors aren't only for children's birthday parties. Adults can give them, too, at special parties. Since party favors usually make up part of the table decoration, it's a good opportunity for imaginative packaging. The Petal Box, shown here (see page 30 for instructions), makes an intriguing wrapping for an oddly shaped gift.

This wrap makes a simple and effective treatment for a party favor, as it even looks a little like a party popper. It can be used for an adult's or child's party. What makes this "instant open" is that fabric has been used, which eliminates the need for tape.

This wrap is great for oddly shaped presents or regularly shaped ones, like the one shown here. Wrap the object in a generous-sized piece of scrap fabric. We fringed the ends of the fabric before wrapping by pulling out threads—this gives the ends some interest. You can also make cuts every quarter-inch or so to make a fringe.

Seal the seam with tape, if you wish, to temporarily hold it. Gather each end with narrow soft ribbon such as satin, grosgrain, or other woven ribbon, and tie into the Basic Bow (see page 35).